SWISS PANORAMA

The most beautiful views
Die schönsten Ansichten der Schweiz
Les plus belles vues de Suisse
美しき風景スイス

Mit Bildern von Christof Sonderegger
und Texten von Patrick Werschler

AT Verlag

46 magnificent panoramic pictures provide a glimpse of Switzerland's natural beauties, variety and lifestyles. They are a souvenir and also an invitation to (re-)visit this picture-perfect land in the heart of Europe.

46 prächtige Panoramabilder geben einen Einblick in die Naturschönheiten und die Vielfalt der Kultur und der Lebensformen der Schweiz. Ein Reiseandenken und zugleich eine Einladung, dieses wunderschöne Land im Herzen Europas (wieder) zu besuchen.

46 vues panoramiques superbes donnent un aperçu des beautés naturelles, de la richesse culturelle et de la diversité des traditions en Suisse. Un souvenir de voyage et une invitation à (re)visiter ce beau pays au cœur de l'Europe.

スイスの自然の美しさ、多様な文化や生活様式を、46枚の豪華パノラマ写真でお届けします。旅の想い出に、また、ヨーロッパの中心にあるこの麗しき国へのいざないとして。

1 Treib
2 Diavolezza
3 Matterhorn
4 Vorderrhein
5 Werdenberg
6 Stein am Rhein
7 Toggenburg
8 La Brévine
9 Lavaux
10 Bern
11 Monte Rosa
12 Jungfraujoch

13 Grand St-Bernard
14 Genève
15 Luzern
16 Bern
17 Aletsch
18 St. Gallen
19 Filisur
20 Thunersee
21 Gruyères
22 Neuchâtel
23 St-Ursanne
24 Schaffhausen

25 Riom
26 Basel
27 Ligerz
28 Morcote
29 Ballenberg
30 Verzasca
31 Basel
32 Bellinzona
33 Appenzell
34 Ascona
35 Chillon
36 Rheinfall

37 Zürich
38 Brunnen
39 Avenches
40 Pilatus
41 Guarda
42 Eiger
43 Emmental
44 Engadin
45 Schöllenen
46 Urnäsch

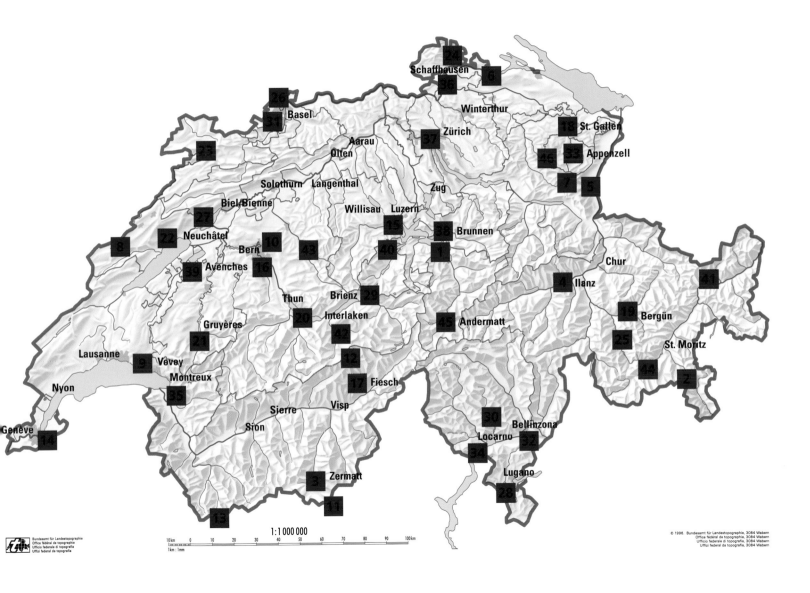

Schaffhausen

Basel

Winterthur

Aarau
Olten

Zürich

St. Gallen

Appenzell

Solothurn
Langenthal

Zug

Biel/Bienne

Willisau
Luzern

Brunnen

Neuchâtel

Bern

Avenches

Chur

Ilanz

Thun

Brienz

Interlaken

Andermatt

Bergün

Gruyères

St. Moritz

Lausanne

Vevey
Montreux

Fiesch

Nyon

Sierre
Visp

Genève

Sion

Bellinzona

Locarno

Lugano

Zermatt

Bundesamt für Landestopographie
Office fédéral de topographie
Ufficio federale di topografia
Uffizi federal da topografia

1:1 000 000

10km   0   10   20   30   40   50   60   70   80   90   100km

1km : 1mm

© 1996. Bundesamt für Landestopographie, 3084 Wabern
Office fédéral de topographie, 3084 Wabern
Ufficio federale di topografia, 3084 Wabern
Uffizi federal da topografia, 3084 Wabern

The old house «zur Treib» at the Lake of Four Cantons, richly-decorated with paintings, used to serve as a shelter for sailors surprised by the strong Föhn winds. Today, the house is a favourite goal for trekkers and day-trippers.

Das alte, mit Malereien reich verzierte Haus zur Treib am Vierwaldstättersee diente früher als Herberge für vom Föhn überraschte Schiffsleute. Heute ist es ein beliebtes Ziel für Wanderer und Ausflügler.

L'ancienne maison «zur Treib» au bord du lac des Quatre Cantons, richement décorée de peintures, servait autrefois de refuge aux bateliers surpris par le foehn. Elle est aujourd'hui un but apprécié des marcheurs et excursionnistes.

この美しく絵画に装飾された古い家は、四森州湖岸のトライブ にある。昔は、フェーンに驚かされた船員達に宿を提供していた。今は、ハイキングや遠足先として人気がある。

The Diavolezza, one of the most
beautiful viewpoints in Switzerland,
is easily reached by aerial cableway.
From there, one can see the impressive
glaciers of the Bernina group from
Piz Palü to Piz Bernina, the eastern-
most 4000-metre peak in the Alps.

Die Diavolezza, einer der schönsten
Aussichtspunkte der Schweiz, ist
bequem mit der Luftseilbahn erreich-
bar. Der Blick geht in die imposante
Gletscherwelt der Berninagruppe,
vom Piz Palü bis zum Piz Bernina, dem
östlichsten Viertausender der Alpen.

La Diavolezza, aisément accessible par
téléphérique, est l'un des plus beaux
points de vue de Suisse. Le regard
porte sur le monde imposant des
glaciers du massif de la Bernina, du
Piz Palü jusqu'au Piz Bernina, le plus
oriental des 4000 des Alpes.

スイスで最も美しい景観のひとつは、
ディアヴォレツァ展望台から。ロープー
ウェイで楽に登れる。東部アルプスの
４千メートル級、ピッツ・パリュから
ピッツ・ベルニナまで、ベルニナ山脈の
堂々たる氷河の世界が広がる。

The Gornergrat (3,130 m) offers a breath-taking view of the Matterhorn, the world's most beautiful mountain. The railway, a pioneering feat of Swiss engineering, leads from Zermatt easily into the heart of the highest peaks in Switzerland.

Den atemberaubendsten Blick aufs Matterhorn, den schönsten Berg der Welt, erhält man vom Gornergrat (3130 m). Die Bahn – eine der Pioniertaten schweizerischer Ingenieurskunst – führt von Zermatt aus bequem mitten ins Herz der höchsten Schweizer Gipfel.

Du Gornergrat (3130 m), on a la vue la plus fascinante sur la plus belle montagne du monde, le Cervin. Ouvrage de pionniers dans l'art des ingénieurs suisses, le train à crémaillère vous emmène de Zermatt au cœur des plus hauts sommets de Suisse.

アッと息をのむ、世界一美しい山、マッターホルンの姿は、**ゴルナーグラート**（3130m）から。スイスの技術工学芸術の先駆けたる登山鉄道で、ツェルマットから楽にスイス最高峰がつらなる真っ只中に到達できる。

The Swiss Grand Canyon is in the Bündner Oberland between Ilanz and Bonaduz. River rafting is a popular activity here as is hiking along the lower Rhine which has had to gnaw its way through the rubble of an ancient rockslide.

Der Grand Canyon der Schweiz liegt im Bündner Oberland, zwischen Ilanz und Bonaduz. Riverrafting ist hier ebenso beliebt wie eine Wanderung entlang des Vorderrheins, der sich durch die Steinmasse eines urzeitlichen Felssturzes fressen musste.

Le Grand Canyon suisse se trouve dans l'Oberland grison, entre Ilanz et Bonaduz. Ici, le rafting est tout aussi apprécié qu'une marche le long du Rhin antérieur. Celui-ci dut se frayer un passage au travers de la masse rocheuse d'un éboulement immémorial.

グラウビュンデンの高地、イランツと
ボナドゥッ間に、スイスのグラン
キャニオンがある。太古の山崩れによる
落岩石に食い入って流れる、フォルデル
ラインは、河沿いのハイキングと共に
河下りでも人気が高い。

Thanks to a legal document granting
it the status of a city, Werdenberg, with
its castle overlooking the idyllic lake,
is the smallest city in Switzerland.
It's a living museum of older, flower-
garlanded wooden buildings crowded
against stone houses.

Werdenberg mit seinem Schloss
über dem idyllischen See ist – dank
eines verbrieften Stadtrechts – die
kleinste Stadt der Schweiz. Als wär's
ein Museum, stehen ältere, blumen-
geschmückte Holzhäuser dicht an
dicht neben den steinernen Häusern
der Betuchteren.

Werdenberg et son château dominant
un lac idyllique est la plus petite
ville de Suisse selon un acte de droit
municipal. Comme dans un musée, de
vieilles maisons de bois décorées de
fleurs se serrent contre celles de pierre
des bourgeois.

保管文書のおかげで都市権をもつスイス
最小の町、**ヴェルデンベルク** と、
牧歌的な湖上に建つ城。博物館のごとく、
花に飾られた古い木造家屋や、もう少し
りっぱな石造の家々が、互いに肩を
寄せ合っている。

The most beautiful of Switzerland's smaller towns, Stein am Rhein is an ancient bridge and border point with row houses and facades decorated with frescoes. It's located near the Untersee where Lake Constance narrows into the Rhine valley.

Am Ende des Untersees verengen sich die weiten Ufer der Bodenseelandschaft zum Tal des Rheins. Dort liegt eine der schönsten Kleinstädte der Schweiz: Stein am Rhein, ein alter Brücken- und Grenzort mit Riegelhäusern und fresekengeschmückten Fassaden.

Au bout du lac Bodan, les vastes rives se resserrent pour devenir la vallée du Rhin abritant l'une des plus jolies petites villes de Suisse, Stein am Rhein, ancien lieu de passage et de frontière, aux maisons à colombages et façades décorées de fresques.

ボーデン湖の広々とした湖畔風景は、ウンター湖の終端になって、ラインの谷へと狭まってゆく。普通は国境となるラインの河向こうながら、スイスに属する古い小さな町、**シュタイン・アム・ライン**。木組み家屋やフレスコ画に飾られた壁面が美しい。

Between the jagged peaks of the
Churfirsten and Appenzell's Alpstein
massif lies the Toggenburg region.
It's a favourite year-round rest and
recreation spot, ideal for hiking and
skiing.

Zwischen den Bergzacken der Churfirsten und dem Massiv des appen-
zellischen Alpsteins ruht das Toggenburg. Im Sommer wie im Winter
ist es ein beliebtes Erholungsgebiet,
ideal für Wanderer und Skifahrer.

Le Toggenburg s'étale entre les pics
des Churfirsten et le massif appenzellois de l'Alpstein. Lieu de villé-
giature apprécié été comme hiver, il
est idéal pour les randonnées et le ski.

クールフィルステンのギザギザの山並みと
アッペンツェルのアルプシュタイン
山脈の間に、**トッゲンブルク** は静かに
横たわる。夏はハイキング、冬はスキーに
最適な、憩の地として好まれる。

La Brévine is known as the Siberia of Switzerland because of its record cold temperatures in winter. But the gentle Jura landscape where La Brévine is situated is anything but cold, extending a warm invitation to relax, hike and cross-country ski.

La Brévine ist wegen der Kälterekorde, die hier immer wieder gemessen werden, bekannt als «schweizerisches Sibirien». Doch die sanfte Juralandschaft, in der La Brévine ruht, ist alles andere als kalt; sie lädt zum Verweilen, Wandern und zum Langlauf.

La Brévine est appelée la «Sibérie suisse» en raison des records de froid qui y sont enregistrés. Le doux paysage du Jura encadrant la Brévine n'a rien de glacial; il invite à la flânerie, la randonnée et le ski de fond.

最低気温の記録更新地であるため、「スイスのシベリア」として知られる**ラ・ブレヴィン**。でも、ここにあるジュラの穏やかな風景は、冷たさとは別個のもの。長期滞在、ハイキングやクロスカントリー・スキーに誘われる。

The sun-drenched, vine-covered slopes of Lavaux stretch between Lausanne and Vevey on Lake Geneva. Visitors are attracted to the wine-making villages by restaurants and the superb view all the way across the lake to the Mont Blanc massif.

Zwischen Lausanne und Vevey am Genfersee dehnen sich die sonnenüberfluteten Hänge des Lavaux aus, vom See bis zu den Hügelkuppen bewachsen mit Rebbergen. In den Weindörfern locken Gaststätten und eine tolle Aussicht – bis hinüber zum Massiv des Mont Blanc.

Entre Lausanne et Vevey, le long du Léman, s'étirent les coteaux inondés de soleil du Lavaux, recouverts de vignes du lac jusqu'aux crêtes. Dans les villages vignerons, d'accueillantes auberges et une vue superbe sur le Mont Blanc vous attendent.

レマン湖畔、ローザンヌとヴヴェの間に、太陽をたっぷり浴びて広がる**ラヴォー** の斜面は、湖から丘の先端まで葡萄畑。モン・ブランまでの素晴しい眺望やレストランは、人々をワインの村々へと招く。

On the second last Monday in November, Bern's Onion Market attracts vegetable growers from far afield to the Swiss capital. Tons of artistically-braided onions are sold and the air is redolent with the odour of onion tart.

Immer am vorletzten Montag im November kommen die Gemüsebauern von weit her nach Bern, in die Hauptstadt der Schweiz. Tonnenweise werden am «Zibelemärit» kunstvoll gefertigte Zwiebelzöpfe verkauft, und über allem liegt der intensive Duft von Zwiebelkuchen.

L'avant-dernier lundi de novembre, les maraîchers venant de loin se rendent à Berne, capitale de la Suisse. Des tonnes de tresses d'oignons artistement nouées sont vendues lors du «Zibelemärit» (marché aux oignons) et partout flotte l'odeur forte des gâteaux aux oignons.

１１月最後から二週目の月曜日には、
遠くからでも野菜農家の人々が、
首都ベルン に集まってくる。芸術的に
編まれた何トンという玉葱の束が
「ツィベレメーリット　（玉葱市）」
で売られ、辺り一面に玉葱パイの
香りが漂う。

The Monte Rosa massif with the Dufourspitze (4,634 m) is the highest point in Switzerland. Six mighty glaciers have flowed for thousands of years between Monte Rosa and the Matterhorn towards the valley and the world famous holiday resort of Zermatt.

Das Monte-Rosa-Massiv mit der Dufourspitze (4634 m) ist die höchste Erhebung der Schweiz. Sechs gewaltige Gletscher fliessen seit Tausenden von Jahren zwischen Monte Rosa und Matterhorn dem Tal und dem welt-berühmten Ferienort Zermatt ent-gegen.

Le massif du Mont Rose avec la Pointe Dufour (4634 m) est le plus haut sommet de Suisse. Six glaciers imposants s'étendent depuis des millénaires entre le Mont Rose et le Cervin face à la vallée et à la célèbre station touristique de Zermatt.

デュフールシュピッツェ（4634m）を有する**モンテ・ローザ** の山並みは、スイス最高の山岳地域。何千年もの昔から6本の巨大な氷河は、モンテ・ローザとマッターホルンの間を谷へ、世界屈指の休暇地ツェルマットの方へと流れている。

The highest mountain railway in Europe leads from Grindelwald up the Kleine Scheidegg to the Jungfraujoch (3,454 m), mostly through the inside of the Eiger. The view of the midlands, the alps and the Aletsch Glacier has to be seen to be believed.

Von Grindelwald auf die Kleine Scheidegg und weiter aufs Jungfraujoch (3454 m) führt, meist im Innern des Eigers, die höchste Bergbahn Europas. Eine grossartigere Sicht auf das Mittelland, die Hochalpen und den Aletschgletscher ist kaum vorstellbar.

Le plus haut chemin de fer d'Europe grimpe de Grindelwald à la Petite Scheidegg et plus haut jusqu'au Jungfraujoch (3454 m), en partie par l'intérieur de l'Eiger. Difficile d'imaginer une vue plus grandiose sur le Moyen Pays, les Hautes Alpes et le glacier d'Aletsch.

グリンデルヴァルトからクライネ・シャイデックを経て、更に**ユングフラウヨッホ**（3454m）へと、ヨーロッパ最高の登山列車はアイガーの中を抜けて行く。ミッテルランド、アルプス、アレッチュ氷河を見渡す景観の壮大さは想像を絶するといえよう。

Hannibal led an army and elephants over the Great St. Bernard against the Romans in 218 BC. The monastery of St. Bernard, founded in the 11th century, has bred the famous St. Bernard dogs for more than 300 years.

Über den Grossen Sankt Bernhard zog schon Hannibal im Jahr 218 v. Chr. mit Elefanten gegen die Römer. Im Kloster, das im 11. Jahrhundert vom heiligen Bernhard gegründet wurde, werden seit über 300 Jahren die berühmten Bernhardinerhunde gezüchtet.

En l'an 218 avant J-C déjà, Hannibal traversa le Grand St-Bernard, marchant avec ses éléphants contre les Romains. L'élevage des célèbres chiens se fait depuis plus de 300 ans dans l'hospice fondé au 11e siècle par Saint-Bernard.

紀元前２１８年、ローマ人に対抗し、ハンニバルは象にまたがり**大サン・ベルナール峠** を越えた。１１世紀に聖ベルンハルトが建てた修道院では、３００年以上前から、名高いセントバーナード犬が飼育されている。

Geneva, at the lower end of Lake Geneva, is the home of many international organizations. The reformer John Calvin worked here and the city state owes its wealth partly to the merchants and bankers seeking refuge from religious persecution.

Genf, am unteren Ende des Genfersees, ist Sitz vieler internationaler Organisationen. Der Reformator Calvin wirkte hier, und der Stadtstaat verdankt seinen Reichtum nicht zuletzt den anderswo wegen ihrer Konfession verfolgten Kaufleuten und Bankiers.

Genève, à l'extrémité inférieure du Léman, est le siège de nombreuses organisations internationales. Le réformateur Calvin y fut actif et la ville-état doit sa richesse aux banquiers et marchands jadis persécutés ailleurs pour leur confession.

レマン湖の最下端に位置するジュネーブ
は、多くの国際機関の所在地。宗教
改革者カルビンのお膝下であり、信仰に
より他で迫害された商人や銀行家が、
町に少なからず富をもたらした。

This metropolis of central Switzerland is situated delightfully at the
outlet of the Lake of Four Cantons.
The mediaeval towers and walls,
richly-decorated houses and the
unique Chapel Bridge and Water
Tower are the highlights of Lucerne.

Luzern ist die Metropole der Inner-
schweiz, herrlich gelegen am Ausfluss
des Vierwaldstättersees. Die mittel-
alterlichen Türme und Stadtmauern,
reich verzierte Herrenhäuser und
die einzigartige Kapellbrücke mit dem
Wasserturm prägen das Stadtbild.

Lucerne, métropole de la Suisse
centrale, jouit d'une belle situation à la
sortie du lac des Quatre Cantons.
Les tours et murailles médiévales, les
maisons richement décorées et le
pont de la Chapelle avec sa tour dans
l'eau caractérisent cette ville.

四森州湖（ルツェルン湖）の流出口に
壮麗に位置する中央スイスの中心都市、
ルツェルン 。中世の塔や市囲壁、
豊富に装飾をほどこされた館、貯水塔を
もつ他に例を見ないカ・ペル橋が、
町の風景を形造る。

The patrician city of Bern became the capital of modern Switzerland in 1848. The mediaeval old city, the famous Clock Tower and the arcades are particularly worth seeing. Bern has been included in the registry of world cultural sites.

Die Patrizierstadt Bern wurde 1848 Hauptstadt der modernen Schweiz. Besonders sehenswert ist die mittelalterliche Altstadt mit dem berühmten Zeitglockenturm und den Lauben. Das gepflegte Stadtbild wurde ins Verzeichnis der Weltkulturgüter aufgenommen.

La cité patricienne de Berne devint en 1848 la capitale de la Suisse moderne. Sa vieille ville médiévale avec sa célèbre Tour de l'Horloge et ses arcades ont un cachet qui leur valut l'inscription aux biens culturels mondiaux.

１８４８年、都市貴族の街であった
ベルン は、現在のスイスの首都と
なった。有名な時計塔やアーケード
のある中世の旧市街が特に見所。
手入れの行き届いた町並は、世界
文化財のリストに列挙されている。

The 24-km length of the Aletsch Glacier makes it the longest glacier in the Alps. It is more than 800 m deep and flows around 200 m a year. Four ice streams join to form this glacier creating three moraines of dark-coloured rocky rubble.

Der Aletschgletscher ist der längste Alpengletscher, 24 km lang und über 800 m tief. Das Eis fliesst pro Jahr rund 200 m. Vier Eisströme vereinigen sich zu diesem Gletscher, darum durch-ziehen ihn drei vom Felsschutt dunkel gefärbte Mittelmoränen.

Le glacier d'Aletsch est le plus long glacier alpin avec ses 24 km de long et plus de 800 m de profondeur. La glace avance d'environ 200 m par an. Quatre fleuves de glace s'unissent pour former ce glacier, dessinant trois moraines médianes sombres faites de déchets de roches.

長さ２４km、深さ８００ｍを越える
アレッチュ はアルプス最長の氷河。
氷は 年に２００ｍ程度移動している。
４本の氷河が合流するため、河には
岩屑で黒ずんだ堆石が３筋走っている。

The abbey of St. Gallen was one of the great centres of learning in Europe in the late Middle Ages. Today, the wonderfully endowed library reflects that greatness. In the 19th century, the city gained world renown for its embroidery and lacework.

Die Abtei Sankt Gallen war im Hochmittelalter eines der ganz grossen europäischen Bildungszentren. Die prachtvoll ausgestattete Stiftsbibliothek zeugt noch heute davon. Seit dem 19. Jahrhundert hat die Stadt Weltruf wegen ihrer Stickereien und Spitzen.

L'abbaye de Saint-Gall fut au haut Moyen Age l'un des grands centres européens de la culture. Sa très riche bibliothèque en témoigne encore aujourd'hui. La ville jouit d'une renommée mondiale depuis le 19e siècle grâce à ses broderies et dentelles.

サンクト・ガレン 僧院は、中世最盛期にはヨーロッパでも指折りの教育機関であった。豪華に仕上げられた図書館が、今日もその面影を偲ばせている。
サンクト・ガレンの刺繍やレースは、
１９世紀以来、世界でも評判が高い。

Before the road network was completed, the Rhaetian Railway was the most important means of transport in Graubünden. The 65 m high Filisur viaduct was regarded as a technical masterpiece when it was built in the early 20th century.

Vor dem Ausbau des Strassennetzes war die Rhätische Bahn das wichtigste Transportmittel Graubündens. Der zu Beginn des 20. Jahrhunderts erbaute 65 m hohe Viadukt bei Filisur galt als technisches Meisterstück schlechthin.

Avant la construction du réseau routier, le chemin de fer Rhétique était le moyen de transport le plus important des Grisons. Le viaduc de Filisur, haut de 65 m et construit au début du 20e siècle, fut considéré comme un pur chef-d'œuvre technique.

道路網が発達するまで、**レーティッシュ鉄道**はグラウビュンデンの最重要交通手段であった。２０世紀初頭にフィリズール近くに建てられた６５ｍの高架橋は、まさに当時の技術的傑作といえよう。

A boat trip on the Lake of Thun is one way of seeing the marvelous variety of the Bernese Oberland mountain landscape. The castle at Oberhofen houses a wide-ranging collection devoted to Bernese lifestyles before 1800.

Eine Schiffahrt auf dem Thunersee gibt einen ersten Einblick in die prächtige und abwechslungsreiche Berglandschaft des Berner Oberlandes. Das Schloss Oberhofen beherbergt eine umfangreiche Sammlung zur bernischen Wohnkultur aus der Zeit vor 1800.

Un tour en bateau sur le lac de Thoune donne une première impression de la majesté des montagnes de l'Oberland bernois. Le château d'Oberhofen abrite une vaste collection sur l'habitat et l'art de vivre avant 1800.

ベルナー・オーバーランドの変化に
富んだ壮大な山々の第一印象は、
トゥーン湖 の遊覧船から。 **オーバー
ホーフェン城** には、１８００年以前の
ベルン生活文化に関する膨大な
コレクションある。

The town of Gruyères, once the ancestral seat of counts, looks today exactly as it did centuries ago. The fortress, the church and residences huddle on their rocky perch. Below the town, the demonstration dairy offers the area's famous cheese.

Das Städtchen Gruyères, einst gräflicher Stammsitz, sieht noch heute genauso aus wie vor Jahrhunderten: Auf dem Felsen thronen die Burg, die Kirche und die Stadthäuser. Unterhalb der Stadt lädt die Schaukäserei zum Probieren des berühmten Käses.

La petite cité de Gruyères, autrefois siège du comté, offre le même visage depuis des siècles. Le château, l'église et les maisons d'habitation trônent sur un rocher. Au pied de la colline, la fromagerie de démonstration invite à déguster le célèbre fromage.

かつて伯爵の在所であった小さな町、グリュイエール 。岩上に城、教会、町の家並が、今も何世紀以前と全く変わらぬ様子で建っている。名産のチーズは、町の下方にある工場で試食できる。

The university city of Neuchâtel controlled the trade route along Lake Neuchâtel for centuries. The vibrant little city nestles between the broad lake and the fortified hill with its castle and Romanesque-Gothic cathedral.

Die Universitätsstadt Neuchâtel beherrschte seit Jahrhunderten die Handelsroute entlang des Neuenburgersees. Die pulsierende Kleinstadt schmiegt sich zwischen den weiten See und den Burghügel mit dem Schloss und der romanisch-gotischen Stiftskirche.

La ville universitaire de Neuchâtel contrôla des siècles durant la route commerciale le long du lac de Neuchâtel. La petite ville trépidante se blottit entre le lac et la colline coiffée du château et de l'église collégiale romano-gothique.

大学町ヌシャテル は、何世紀も前から
ヌシャテル湖畔の商いルートを支配して
きた。城やロマネスク・ゴシック様式の
僧院教会が建つ丘と広い湖との間に
ピッタリはまって、小さな町は脈打つ。

St-Ursanne, a small town on the Doubs River in the Jura region, boasts a remarkable late Romanesque church, a city gate with the best-preserved example of Burgundian carving and an old stone bridge bedecked with statues.

St-Ursanne, das kleine Jurastädtchen am Doubs, hat nicht nur eine bemerkenswerte spätromanische Stiftskirche, sondern unter seinen Stadttoren auch das besterhaltene Tor aus burgundischem Schnitzwerk und eine mit Statuen geschmückte alte Steinbrücke.

St-Ursanne, petite cité le long du Doubs, possède une admirable collégiale de style roman tardif, des portes de ville dont fait partie la représentante la mieux conservée de l'art sculpté bourguignon ainsi qu'un vieux pont de pierre décoré de statues.

ドゥ川のほとりにあるジュラ地方の
こぢんまりとした町、 **サンテュル
サン** 。後期ロマネスク様式の教会は
もとより、よく保存されたブルゴーニュの
彫刻入りの街門や、彫像に飾られた古い
石橋も注目に値する。

The landmark in Schaffhausen is the
Munot, a mighty fortress. Formerly
a free city of the empire, Schaffhausen
profited from its favourable position
as a bridgehead and a transfer centre
for the transport of goods blocked
by the nearby Rhine Falls.

Das Wahrzeichen Schaffhausens ist
der Munot, eine mächtige Befesti-
gungsanlage. Die frühere freie Reichs-
stadt profitierte stets von ihrer
günstigen Lage als Brückenkopf und
Umschlagplatz des Warentransports,
der durch den nahen Rheinfall
behindert wurde.

L'imposante forteresse du Munot
est l'emblème de Schaffhouse. Jadis
ville impériale libre, elle profita
toujours de sa situation de tête de pont
et de lieu de transbordement des
marchandises dont le transport était
entravé par les chutes du Rhin
toutes proches.

ムノートと呼ばれる、がっしりとした
防備施設が、**シャフハウゼン** の象徴。
この元帝国直属自由都市は、ラインの
対岸にあり、且つ、荷の積み替えが
必要となる滝の手前という土地柄を
活用してきた。

25

The typical Graubünden landscape (here in Riom near Savognin) consists of deeply-etched river valleys, above which lie gently rising plateaus. The human presence is marked by scattered settlements and compact villages, white walls gleaming in the sun.

Die typische Landschaft Graubündens (hier in Riom bei Savognin) besteht aus tief eingeschnittenen Flusstälern, über denen sanft ansteigende Hoch-plateaus liegen. Die Kulturlandschaft ist geprägt von Streusiedlungen und kompakten, in der Sonne weiss leuchtenden Dörfern.

Le paysage typique des Grisons (ici à Riom près de Savognin) se compose de vallées fluviales profondes surmontées de hauts-plateaux aux pentes douces. Habitations disséminées et villages compacts, tout blancs dans le soleil, se détachent sur fond de terres cultivées.

深く刻まれた渓谷と、その上方に
緩やかに登り坂となって広がる高原は、
グラウビュンデンの典型的な景観
(写真はサヴォニン近郊のリオム)。
散在する農家や密集した白壁が陽に
輝く村々が、開拓の跡を刻む。

26

A leading trade and university centre since the Middle Ages, Basel also has time for fun during Carnival. The exuberant and poetic three days of madness begin at 4 a.m. with the «Morgestraich» followed by colourful processions.

Basel, seit dem Mittelalter eine führende Handels- und Universitäts-stadt, weiss den Karneval besonders ausgelassen und poetisch zu feiern. Frühmorgens um vier beginnt das dreitägige närrische Treiben mit dem «Morgestraich», gefolgt von farbigen Umzügen.

Bâle, éminente cité commerciale et universitaire depuis le Moyen Age, sait fêter le carnaval d'une manière parti-culièrement exubérante et poétique. Le «Morgestraich» amorce à quatre heures du matin la folle animation de trois jours et ses cortèges colorés.

中世の頃から主要な商業地で、大学町の一つでもあったバーゼル 。カーニバルは、格別奔放かつ詩的に祝う。 3 日にわたるバカ騒ぎは、早朝 4 時の「モルゲシュトライヒ」と呼ばれる合図に始まり、色鮮やかなパレードが続く。

It is a magnificent and peaceful view from the vineyards on the Lake of Biel above the former pilgrimage church at Ligerz. Across the lake and the idyllic Saint Peter's Island, rise green hills and the whole alpine panorama.

Die Aussicht von den Rebbergen am Bielersee, hier oberhalb der früheren Wallfahrtskirche bei Ligerz, ist gleichzeitig beruhigend und erhaben. Über dem See und der idyllischen Sankt-Peters-Insel erheben sich grüne Hügelkuppen und das ganze Alpen-panorama.

La vue du haut des coteaux du lac de Bienne, ici au-dessus de l'ancienne église de pèlerinage de Ligerz, est à la fois apaisante et grandiose. Les coupoles vertes des collines et tout le panorama des Alpes dominent le lac et l'île St-Pierre idyllique.

昔は巡礼札所であった **リゲルツ** 教会の上方、葡萄地からの眺望は、心安らかで気高い。湖と牧歌的なサンクト・ペーター半島の背後には、丸い丘並み、そして、壮大なアルプスのパノラマが広がる。

Morcote, nestled between water
and mountains, is one of the most
picturesque towns on Lake Lugano.
Ticinese handicrafts are on sale under
the town's arcades. 400 steps lead
to the church of Maria del Sasso. The
marvelous view is worth the sweaty
climb.

Eines der malerischsten Uferdörfer
am Luganersee, eingezwängt zwischen
Wasser und Berg, ist Morcote. Unter
Arkaden wird Tessiner Kunsthand-
werk angeboten, und die 400 Stufen
zur Kirche Maria del Sasso bringen
viel Schweiss, aber auch eine prächtige
Aussicht.

Morcote, l'un des villages riverains
les plus pittoresques du lac de Lugano,
se blottit entre eau et montagne.
Sous les arcades, on trouve des objets
d'artisanat tessinois. Les 400 marches
conduisant à l'église Maria del Sasso
mettent en sueur, mais pour une
vue magnifique.

水と山に挟まれ、ルガノ湖畔に絵の
ごとくたたずむ村、モルコーテ。
アーケードの下では、ティチーノ（伊系
スイス）の民芸品が並ぶ。マリア・デル・
サッソ教会へと四百段を登ると、たっぷり
汗をかかされるが、眺めは素晴しい。

29

The open-air museum of Ballenberg above the wood-carving centre of Brienz is an adventure park devoted to rural lifestyles. Farmhouses from all over Switzerland have been brought to the large area where they have been opened to visitors.

Ein Erlebnispark der ländlichen Wohnkultur ist das Freilichtmuseum Ballenberg oberhalb Brienz, dem Holz-schnitzlerdorf. Bauernhäuser aus der ganzen Schweiz wurden hier wieder aufgebaut und können in einer weiten Parklandschaft bestaunt und betreten werden.

Le musée en plein air de Ballenberg au-dessus de Brienz, patrie des sculp-teurs sur bois, permet de découvrir l'habitat rural. Des fermes de toute la Suisse ont été rebâties à cet endroit. Elles peuvent être admirées et visitées dans un très vaste parc.

木彫りで有名な村ブリエンツの上方
には、田舎の生活様式を体験できる
屋外博物館、**バレンベルク** がある。
スイス全国から運び込んだ農家を
広い公園内に再現。それぞれ中に入る
ことができ、賛嘆させられる。

The Verzasca Valley is dark green water, grey granite, foaming white waterfalls and natural pools offering an invitation to swim. The path through this side valley in Ticino leads across this twin-arched bridge near Lavertezzo.

Tiefgrünes Wasser, grauer Granit und weiss schäumende Wasserfälle, aber auch natürliche Tümpel, die zum Bade laden, finden sich im Verzascatal. Der Saumpfad durch dieses Tessiner Seitental führte über diese Brücke mit dem Doppelbogen bei Lavertezzo.

Dans le val Verzasca, l'eau est d'un vert profond, le granite gris et l'écume des cascades blanche. Des mares naturelles y invitent à la baignade. Le sentier qui traversait cette vallée latérale passait par ce pont à double arche près de Lavertezzo.

ヴェルツァスカ谷 には、深い緑の水流、灰色の花崗岩、白く泡立つ滝、そして自然にできた水浴場もある。ラヴェルテッツォ付近にあるこの眼鏡橋を越えて、細い山道は谷の奥へと続く。

Basel is known for the quality and variety of its cultural scene. The Tinguely Fountain at the city theatre is a charming contrast to the Neo-gothic Elisabethen Church. Cold winter weather continues the fantasy of the artist.

Basel ist bekannt für die Vielfalt und Qualität seines kulturellen Angebots. Der Tinguely-Brunnen vor dem Stadt-theater bildet einen reizvollen Kontrast zur neugotischen Elisabethenkirche. Die Winterkälte führt die Phantasie des Künstlers auf ihre Weise weiter.

Bâle est connue pour la polyvalence et la qualité de sa culture. La fontaine de Tinguely devant le théâtre muni-cipal crée un contraste étonnant avec l'église élisabéthaine néogothique. Le gel prolonge à sa façon la fantaisie de l'artiste.

文化の多面性と質の良さで知られる
バーゼル。市立劇場前の **タングリ泉** は、
新ゴシック様式のエリザベート教会と
魅惑的な対照をなす。冬の寒さが、
芸術家のファンタジーを更に発展させて
いるようだ。

32

Bellinzona's charm as the capital of
Ticino is in the contrast between the
three walled fortresses on the cliffs
and the refined old town which in turn
competes with postmodern architecture of international standing.

Der Charme Bellinzonas, der Tessiner
Hauptstadt, liegt im Kontrast zwischen
den drei befestigten Burgen auf den
Felsen und der gepflegten Altstadt, die
ihrerseits im spannenden Wettbewerb
mit postmoderner Architektur von
Weltgeltung steht.

Le charme de Bellinzone, chef-lieu
du Tessin, réside dans le contraste
entre les trois châteaux forts sur les
rochers et la vieille ville soignée qui
rivalise pour sa part avec l'architecture
postmoderne à réputation mondiale.

ティチーノの首都、ベリンツォーナ 。
岩上に建つ強固たる３つの城と手入れが
行き届いた旧市街とのコントラスト、
旧市街と世界的評価を受けるポスト・
モダンな建築との緊張感ある競合、
にその魅力がある。

33

The traditional rural lifestyle is still strong in Appenzell. In the autumn, the herdsmen continue to put on their colourful Sunday best when they drive their cows and goats down from the alpine meadows back to their winter quarters.

Die traditionelle bäuerliche Lebensart wird in Appenzell noch immer grossgeschrieben. Die Sennen legen ihre farbenfrohe Sonntagstracht an, wenn sie im Herbst die Kühe und Ziegen von den saftigen Alpweiden zurück in ihre angestammten Höfe treiben.

Le style de vie paysan traditionnel a toujours ses lettres de noblesse à Appenzell. En automne, les vachers revêtent leur costume du dimanche haut en couleurs lorsqu'ils ramènent vaches et chèvres des gras pâturages dans leurs quartiers d'hiver.

伝統的な農家の生活様式が、**アッペン ツェル** では今も尚大事にされている。 秋、酪農家は色鮮やかな晴れ着をまとい、 牛や山羊をみずみずしい高原から 先祖伝来の農場へと連れ帰る。

Ascona used to be a fishing village. It is beautifully situated and fits exactly into the cliché image of mild climates and southern lifestyles. Today a chic international meeting place, it attracted at all times famous artists, philosophers and bohemians.

Das ehemalige Fischerdorf Ascona ist wunderschön gelegen und entspricht genau dem Clichébild von südländischer Lebensart und mildem Klima. Der heute mondäne internationale Treffpunkt zog immer schon namhafte Künstler, Philosophen und Bohémiens an.

Ancien village de pêcheurs, Ascona jouit d'une situation magnifique, conforme au cliché du climat doux et du mode de vie méridional. Aujourd'hui lieu de rencontre international mondain, il attira toujours artistes célèbres, philosophes et farfelus.

元漁村の**アスコーナ** は、素晴しく美しい土地柄にあり、イメージ通り、南国風な生活様式や温暖な気候を満喫させてくれる。この優雅な国際町には、名高い芸術家や哲学者、因習にとらわれぬ自由人達が集まる。

35

The castle of Chillon, perched on
a rocky outcrop on the shore of Lake
Geneva near Montreux, is the most
impressive and best preserved lake-
side castle in Switzerland. In the late
Middle Ages it was the favoured
residence of the Counts of Savoy.

In der Nähe von Montreux thront auf
einem Felsen am Ufer des Genfersees
Schloss Chillon. Das beeindruckendste
und besterhaltene Wasserschloss der
Schweiz war im späten Mittelalter
der Lieblingssitz der mächtigen Grafen
von Savoyen.

Non loin de Montreux, le château
de Chillon trône sur un rocher au bord
du lac Léman. Le plus impressionnant
et le mieux conservé des châteaux
lacustres de Suisse fut, à la fin du
Moyen Age, la résidence préférée des
puissants comtes de Savoie.

モントルー近く、レマン湖畔の岩上に
君臨する、**シヨン城**。このスイスで最も
よく保存され印象深い、水に囲まれた
古城は、中世末期に権勢をもった
サボイ諸侯に愛された。

The Rhine Falls at Neuhausen is the largest rapids in Europe. The river drops 25 m. The rocks in the middle of the river and the boat crowded with tourists almost disappear in the rising mist.

Der Rheinfall bei Neuhausen ist die gewaltigste Stromschnelle Europas; 25 Meter stürzt der Rhein in die Tiefe. Die Felsen in der Flussmitte und die Boote mit den bangenden Touristen verschwinden beinahe ganz in den auf-steigenden Gischtschwaden.

Les chutes du Rhin près de Neuhausen sont les plus imposantes d'Europe; le Rhin s'y jette d'une hauteur de 25 m. Les rochers au milieu du fleuve et les bateaux chargés de touristes ébahis disparaissent quasiment dans les voiles d'embruns.

ノイハウゼン近くにある**ラインの滝** の強大さはヨーロッパ随一。ここで２５ｍラインは流れ落ちる。河の真ん中にある岩も、心配気な観光客を乗せたボートも、どんどん高まる水飛沫に消えて行きそうだ。

Zürich, the economic centre of
Switzerland, offers not only the famous
Bahnhofstrasse and its chic shops, but
also a romantic old city, the mansions
of wealthy businessmen along the
Limmat and a wealth of culture.

Die Wirtschaftsmetropole Zürich
besteht nicht nur aus der berühmten
Bahnhofstrasse mit ihren mondänen
Geschäften. Sie bietet in der Altstadt
manch romantischen Winkel, von
reichen Kaufleuten erbaute Herrenhäuser an der Limmat und viel,
viel Kultur.

Zurich, métropole économique, n'est
pas faite que de la célèbre Bahnhofstrasse aux magasins mondains.
Cité de culture, sa vieille ville recèle
nombre de recoins romantiques et des
maisons bourgeoises bâties le long
de la Limmat par de riches marchands.

経済の中心地チューリヒ にあるのは、
上流店の並ぶ有名なバーンホーフ通り
ばかりではない。旧市街には、多くの
ロマンティックな町角、リマト川岸には、
裕福な商人が建てた館があり、文化が
あふれている。

38

The rail trip up the Urmiberg above Brunnen offers the best view of the cradle of Switzerland. On the far shore of the deep blue Lake of Four Cantons is the Rütli meadow where in 1291 the Swiss Confederation was founded.

Einen Blick auf die Wiege der Schweiz erhält, wer die Bahn auf den Urmiberg ob Brunnen nimmt. Der Vierwaldstättersee liegt tiefblau da; auf der anderen Seeseite ist die Rütliwiese sichtbar, wo 1291 die Eidgenossenschaft gegründet wurde.

Celui qui emprunte la télécabine montant sur l'Urmiberg au-dessus de Brunnen peut voir le berceau de la Suisse. Le lac des Quatre Cantons s'étale, d'un bleu profond; en face, on aperçoit la prairie du Grütli où la Confédération fut fondée en 1291.

ブルンネンからロープーウェイで
ウルミベルク に登ると、スイスの発祥地
を一目に収めることができる。四森州湖が
青く深く横たわり、その向こう岸には
リュトゥリの緑地が見える。ここに
１２９１年、スイス連邦が成立した。

39

The mediaeval town of Avenches near Lake Murten was known as Aventicum in Roman times. It was the capital of Helvetia and was considerably bigger, with thermal bathes and an amphitheatre. Today, the amphitheatre is the site of annual festivals.

Das mittelalterliche Städtchen Avenches in der Nähe des Murtensees war zur Römerzeit unter dem Namen Aventicum Hauptstadt von Helvetien. Es war wesentlich grösser, besass Thermen und ein Amphitheater. Im Amphitheater finden nun jedes Jahr Festspiele statt.

La petite cité médiévale d'Avenches, près du lac de Morat, était la capitale de l'Helvétie romaine sous le nom d'Aventicum. Nettement plus grande, elle possédait des thermes et un amphithéâtre où un festival a lieu chaque année de nos jours.

ムルテン湖の近くにある中世の町 **アヴァンシュ** は、ローマ時代にはヘルヴェ ティア地方の首都で、アヴェンティクムと よばれ、明らかにもっと大きく、 温泉や円形劇場も有した。その円形 劇場では、記念公演が毎年行われる。

There are two ways to travel up the Pilatus – by cable car or cogwheel railway. The geographical centre of Switzerland overlooks Lucerne, the twisting arms of the Lake of Four Cantons, the green, rolling midlands and the whole Alpine range.

Zwei Bahnen führen auf den Pilatus, eine Seilbahn und eine Zahnrad-bahn. Aus der geografischen Mitte der Schweiz schweift der Blick auf Luzern, die gewundenen Wasserarme des Vierwaldstättersees, das grüne, hüge-lige Mittelland und den ganzen Alpenbogen.

Un téléphérique et un train à cré-maillère conduisent au sommet du Pilate. Du haut du centre géographique de la Suisse, le regard porte sur Lucerne, les bras tortueux du lac des Quatre Cantons, le Moyen Pays aux vertes collines et tout l'arc alpin.

ピラトゥス には、ロープーウェイか
歯車起動の登山電車で登ることができる。
地理的にスイスの中央に位置し、
頂上からは、ルツェルン、四森州湖の
曲がりくねった支流、ミッテルランドの
緑の丘陵地、そしてアルプス山脈の
全貌が見渡せる。

Guarda is the most beautiful village in the lower Engadine with its whitewashed stone houses decorated with wonderful designs. It is also a good example of how old cultural sites can be preserved without turning them into museums.

Guarda ist mit seinen weiss getünchten Steinhäusern, verziert mit prächtigen Graffiti, wohl das schönste Unterengadiner Dorf. Es ist auch ein Musterbeispiel dafür, dass altes Kulturgut bewahrt werden kann, ohne dass das Dorf zu einem Museum wird.

Guarda est certainement le plus joli village de la Basse Engadine, avec ses maisons de pierre blanchies et décorées de superbes graffitis. C'est aussi un modèle exemplaire de conservation des biens culturels sans transformation du village en musée.

白い漆喰に鮮やかな模様が描かれた
石造りの家々がある**グアルダ** は、ウンター
エンガディンで一番美しい村といえよう。
この村は、博物館にせずとも、古い
文化財を守ることができることを示す、
よい例でもある。

42

These are the three stars of the
Bernese Alps. Ever since daring British
climbers first faced their challenges,
these peaks have lost none of their
fascination. The Eiger north face
is one of the most difficult ascents
anywhere.

Eiger, Mönch und Jungfrau gelten als
das Dreigestirn der Berner Alpen.
Seit wagemutige Engländer begannen,
die Alpengipfel zu erklimmen, hat
ihre Faszination nicht nachgelassen.
Die Eigernordwand ist eine der schwie-
rigsten Kletterrouten überhaupt.

L'Eiger, le Mönch et la Jungfrau sont
les stars des Alpes bernoises. Depuis
que d'audacieux Anglais se mirent
à escalader les sommets alpins, leur
fascination n'a pas diminué. La paroi
nord de l'Eiger est l'une des voies
d'ascension les plus difficiles.

ベルナーアルプスの三大山と名を馳せる、
アイガー、メンヒ、ユングフラウ。
大胆不敵な英国人が、アルプス登頂を
目指して以来、その情熱は衰えることが
ない。アイガー北壁は、まさに最難関
ルートのひとつだ。

Emmental is the home of the most famous of the Swiss cheeses. The green valleys and steep hills are ideally suited for dairy farming. Typical of the architecture are the farmhouses and the broadly overhanging roofs to protect against wind and weather.

Die Heimat des berühmtesten Schweizer Käses ist das Emmental. Die Landschaft mit grünen Tälern und steilen Hügelkuppen ist wie gemacht für die Milchwirtschaft. Typisch sind die Bauernhäuser mit weit ausladenden, vor Wind und Wetter schützenden Dächern.

La patrie du plus célèbre fromage suisse est l'Emmental. Ce paysage aux vertes vallées et collines à sommets escarpés semble prédestiné à l'économie laitière. Ses fermes typiques déploient de vastes toits protégeant du vent et des intempéries.

最もよく知られたスイス産チーズの故郷、**エメンタール** 。緑の谷や起伏の激しい丘陵地は、酪農のために作られたようなもの。風や悪天候を防ぐために広く突き出した屋根は、この地方の農家に典型的だ。

The lake region of the Upper Engadine – here at Sils – offers rest and relaxation for body and soul. For the more actively inclined, there is a variety of sports: hiking, sailing, riding, cross country skiing and ice skating.

Die Oberengadiner Seenlandschaft – hier bei Sils – verspricht Ruhe und Erholung für Körper und Geist. Aber auch wer gerne Sport treibt, kommt hier auf die Rechnung, sei es beim Wandern, Segeln oder Reiten, im Winter beim Skilanglauf und beim Eislaufen.

La région des lacs en Haute Engadine – ici près de Sils – promet calme et repos pour le corps et l'esprit. Mais celui qui aime le sport y trouve aussi son compte dans les domaines de la marche, la voile ou l'équitation, en hiver le ski de fond et le patinage.

ここ**シルス**に見られるような、オーバーエンガディンの湖水風景は、心身共に休養・安らぎを与えてくれる。また、スポーツをしたい人には、ハイキング、ヨット、乗馬、冬にはスキーやスケートと、期待を裏切らない。

45

The Furka-Oberalp Railway wends
its way through the wild and romantic
Schoellenen Gorge between Goesche-
nen and Andermatt at the Gotthard
Pass. According to local legend, the
first bridge over the Schoellenen is said
to have been built by the devil.

Die Furka Oberalp Bahn windet
sich durch die wildromantische
Schöllenenschlucht zwischen Göschenen und Andermatt am Gotthard-
pass. Die erste Brücke über die Schöllenen soll der Teufel gebaut haben,
erzählt die Sage.

Le train Furka-Oberalp se tortille
à travers les gorges sauvages et romantiques des Schöllenen entre Göschenen
et Andermatt sur le tracé du Gotthard.
Selon la légende, le diable en aurait
construit le premier pont.

ゴットハルト峠の麓、フルカ・オーバー
アルプ鉄道は、ゲシェネンと
アンデルマット間にある野性的ロマンに
満ちた**シェッレネン渓谷** を蛇行して進む。
伝説によると、この渓谷最初の橋は
悪魔の仕業。

46

With a deafening drone, cowbells ring in the New Year in Urnäsch in the Appenzell hinterland. The huge, elaborate masks of the Silvesterkläuse are meant only to chase evil spirits, but maybe they also frighten the onlookers.

Ohrenbetäubend dröhnen die Kuhschellen zum Jahreswechsel durch Urnäsch im Appenzeller Hinterland. Und die kunstvollen, gewaltigen Masken der Silvesterkläuse – machen sie nur den bösen Geistern Angst, oder lehren sie auch die Zuschauer das Fürchten?

Les sonnailles assourdissantes retentissent à Urnäsch, dans l'arrière-pays appenzellois, pour fêter l'an nouveau. Les énormes masques de la St-Sylvestre, artistement décorés, effraient-ils seulement les mauvais esprits ou aussi les spectateurs?

年の変わり目には、耳をつんざくような牛の鐘音がアッペンツェル奥地のウルネシュ から響いてくる。サンタならぬ大晦日クロースの技巧をこらしたとてつもない仮面。悪霊を恐れさせるためだけなのか、見物客を怖がらせるものなのか？

Die Fotos wurden mit einer Noblex Mittelformat-Panoramakamera
mit einem Bildwinkel von 140° aufgenommen.

Die Karte auf Seite 3 wurde reproduziert mit Bewilligung
des Bundesamtes für Landestopographie vom 9.6.1997.

Übersetzungen:
Englisch: Paul Sufrin, Toronto
Französisch: Carmen Scherrer, Château-d'Oex
Japanisch: Urs und Tamami Loosli, Herrliberg

6. Auflage, 2006

© 1997
AT Verlag, 5001 Aarau, Schweiz
Lithos: Fotolito Longo, Bozen
Druck und Bindearbeiten: Westermann Druck, Zwickau
Printed in Germany

ISBN 3-85502-596-7
ISBN 978-3-85502-596-1